To Stephanie

A NOTE FROM THE AUTHOR

In his *Book of Woodcraft* the great naturalist Ernest Thompson Seton listed forty birds that he thought every child should know. Though I disagreed with some of his selections, the listing made me think: How many and which birds should every child know? Which fish? Which mammals? What other animals?

The four books in the series CRINKLEROOT'S 100 ANIMALS EVERY CHILD SHOULD KNOW (*Crinkleroot's 25 Birds, 25 Fish, 25 Mammals*, and *25 More Animals*) are intended to provide a base of knowledge of the animal kingdom. I hope my selections will make parents and teachers consider, as Mr. Seton's forty birds made me consider, which other animals should be included.

—Jim Arnosky

Bradbury Press
Macmillan Publishing Company
866 Third Avenue
New York, NY 10022

Maxwell Macmillan Canada, Inc.
1200 Eglinton Avenue East
Suite 200
Don Mills, Ontario M3C 3N1

Macmillan Publishing Company is part of the
Maxwell Communication Group of Companies.

First edition
Printed and bound in the United States of America
10 9 8 7 6 5 4 3 2 1
The text is set in ITC Bookman Light. Typography by Julie Quan

Printed on recycled paper

LIBRARY OF CONGRESS CATALOGING-IN-PUBLICATION DATA
Arnosky, Jim.
Crinkleroot's 25 mammals every child should know / by Jim Arnosky.—
1st ed.
p.   cm.
Summary: The jovial woodsman Crinkleroot introduces twenty-five realistically drawn mammals, including the dog, beaver, and elephant.
ISBN 0-02-705845-X
1. Mammals—Juvenile literature.   2. Mammals—Identification—Juvenile literature.   [1. Mammals.]   I. Title.   II. Title:
Crinkleroot's twenty-five mammals every child should know.
QL706.2.A76   1994
599—dc20   93-7585

Crinkleroot's

25 MAMMALS

EVERY CHILD SHOULD KNOW

BY JIM ARNOSKY

BRADBURY PRESS   NEW YORK

Maxwell Macmillan Canada   Toronto
Maxwell Macmillan International
New York   Oxford   Singapore   Sydney

Hello! My name is Crinkleroot. Like you, I'm a human being. I'm also a mammal. So are you!

Mammals are animals who, as babies, feed on mothers' milk.

Do you know any other kinds of mammals besides humans? In this book there are twenty-five mammals you should know.

Mammals come in all kinds of different shapes and sizes.

Mammal youngsters stay with their parents
a very long time. They leave to live on
their own only after they have grown big enough
and smart enough to take care of themselves.

Mammals like to play. In their play they
practice the important survival skills
of running, hiding, hunting,
and finding food.

Have fun learning your mammals!

Your friend,

Crinkleroot

Human

Dog

Cat

Squirrel

Mouse

Horse

Cow

Pig

Deer

Sheep

Bear

Raccoon

Skunk

Beaver

Bat

Rabbit

Fox

Wolf

Lion

Tiger

Kangaroo

Elephant

Whale

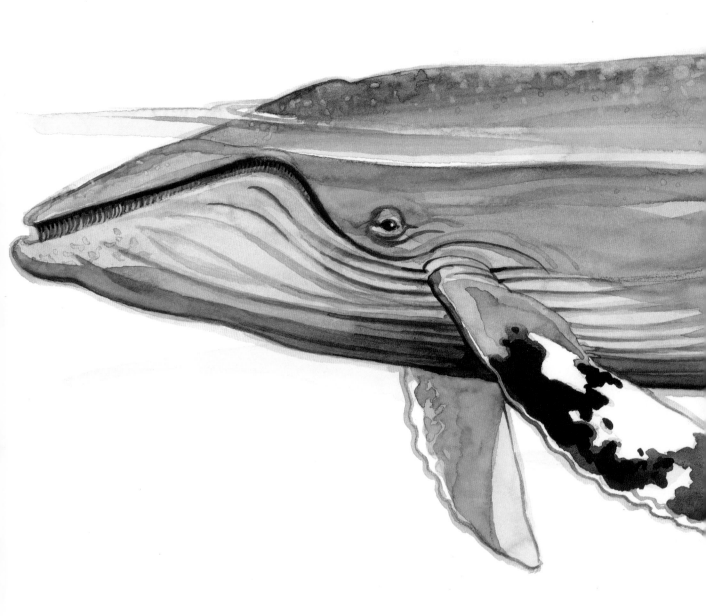

Monkey